# 故園畫憶

庚寅中秋
韓磐陸題

**《故园画忆系列》编委会**

**名誉主任**：韩启德

**主　　任**：邵　鸿

**委　　员**：（按姓氏笔画为序）

|  |  |  |  |
|---|---|---|---|
| 万　捷 | 王秋桂 | 方李莉 | 叶培贵 |
| 刘魁立 | 况　晗 | 严绍璗 | 吴为山 |
| 范贻光 | 范　芳 | 孟　白 | 邵　鸿 |
| 岳庆平 | 郑培凯 | 唐晓峰 | 曹兵武 |

故园画忆系列
Memory of the Old Home in Sketches

# 天山北部风情

## Style in North of Tianshan Mountains

李钦曾 罗丹 绘画 撰文
Sketches & Notes by Li Qinzeng Luo Dan

学苑出版社
ACADEMY PRESS

## 图书在版编目（CIP）数据

天山北部风情 / 李钦曾, 罗丹绘画、撰文. — 北京：学苑出版社，2017.8
（故园画忆系列）
ISBN 978-7-5077-5304-2

Ⅰ.①天… Ⅱ.①李…②罗… Ⅲ.①钢笔画—作品集—中国—现代②新疆—概况 Ⅳ.①J224.8②K924.5

中国版本图书馆CIP数据核字（2017）第215403号

| | |
|---|---|
| 出 版 人： | 孟　白 |
| 责任编辑： | 洪文雄　周　鼎 |
| 出版发行： | 学苑出版社 |
| 社　　址： | 北京市丰台区南方庄2号院1号楼 |
| 邮政编码： | 100079 |
| 网　　址： | www.book001.com |
| 电子信箱： | xueyuanpress@163.com |
| 联系电话： | 010-67601101（营销部）、67603091（总编室） |
| 经　　销： | 全国新华书店 |
| 印 刷 厂： | 北京赛文印刷有限公司 |
| 开本尺寸： | 889×1194　1/24 |
| 印　　张： | 5 |
| 字　　数： | 130千字 |
| 图　　幅： | 95幅 |
| 版　　次： | 2017年8月北京第1版 |
| 印　　次： | 2017年8月北京第1次印刷 |
| 定　　价： | 48.00元 |

# 目　录

自　序　　　　　　　　　　　　李钦曾

## 历史建筑

| | |
|---|---|
| 迪化城 | 3 |
| 老满城·民居 | 4 |
| 老满城·鼓楼 | 5 |
| 亚尔果勒村·正门 | 6 |
| 亚尔果勒村·小巷 | 7 |
| 六星街·俄式民居 | 8 |
| 六星街·装饰局部 | 9 |
| 离街·二层小楼 | 10 |
| 离街·宅院大门 | 11 |
| 离街·街角 | 12 |
| 离街·维吾尔族民居 | 13 |
| 离街·回族民居 | 14 |
| 离街·乌孙邮局 | 15 |
| 红山宝塔 | 16 |
| 伊犁将军府 | 17 |
| 陕西回族大寺 | 18 |
| 老油坊 | 19 |
| 奇台古城窖·墙面 | 20 |
| 奇台古城窖·酿酒工具 | 21 |
| 塔尔阿特麻扎 | 22 |
| 卵石墓 | 23 |
| 切木尔切克墓地 | 24 |
| 阿敦乔鲁石堆墓 | 25 |
| 科克舍木老克木齐石人 | 26 |
| 阿贡盖提草原石人阵 | 27 |
| 喀让格托海石人 | 28 |

## 乡土建筑

| | |
|---|---|
| 维吾尔族民居·建筑群 | 31 |
| 维吾尔族民居·平房 | 32 |
| 维吾尔族民居·院落 | 33 |
| 维吾尔族民居·大门 | 34 |
| 维吾尔族民居·檐廊 | 35 |
| 葡萄沟 | 36 |
| 葡萄干晾房·全景 | 37 |
| 葡萄干晾房·墙体 | 38 |
| 清真寺塔楼 | 39 |

| | | | |
|---|---|---|---|
| 坎儿井 | 40 | 地窝子·大门 | 67 |
| 涝坝 | 41 | 干打垒房子 | 68 |
| 伊犁河·栈道 | 42 | | |
| 伊犁河·木桥 | 43 | **民风民俗** | |
| 大西沟 | 44 | 逛巴扎的人 | 71 |
| 喀拉峻草原 | 45 | 逛巴扎的人 | 72 |
| 冬窝子·全景 | 46 | 修鞋匠 | 73 |
| 冬窝子·墙面 | 47 | 打铁匠 | 74 |
| 冬窝子·转场 | 48 | 转场队伍 | 75 |
| 冬窝子·废墟 | 49 | 转场牧民 | 76 |
| 哈萨克族村庄·全景 | 50 | 牧民与马 | 77 |
| 哈萨克族村庄·民居 | 51 | 骑马少年 | 78 |
| 哈萨克族村庄·石头墙 | 52 | 驯鹰人 | 79 |
| 哈萨克族村庄·栅栏 | 53 | 筛谷物的人 | 80 |
| 哈萨克族村庄·羊圈 | 54 | 养蜂人 | 81 |
| 哈萨克族村庄·牲口棚 | 55 | 蜂房 | 82 |
| 哈萨克族毡房·外景 | 56 | 制奶酒 | 83 |
| 哈萨克族毡房·内景 | 57 | 喝奶酒 | 84 |
| 蒙古族营地·全景 | 58 | 奶酒的仪式 | 85 |
| 蒙古族营地·蒙古包 | 59 | 敖包祭祀 | 86 |
| 蒙古族营地·小屋 | 60 | 婚礼 | 87 |
| 蒙古族营地·室外厨房 | 61 | 麦西热甫 | 88 |
| 图瓦人民居·村落 | 62 | 且力西 | 89 |
| 图瓦人民居·建筑 | 63 | 斗羊 | 90 |
| 图瓦人民居·院子 | 64 | 仪礼歌 | 91 |
| 地窝子·近景 | 65 | 奎依 | 92 |
| 地窝子·大门 | 66 | 卡拉角勒哈 | 93 |

| | | | |
|---|---|---|---|
| 哈萨克族毡房制作技艺 | 94 | 帕拉斯制作技艺 | 98 |
| 刺绣技艺·维吾尔族 | 95 | 红柳条编织技艺 | 99 |
| 刺绣技艺·哈萨克族 | 96 | 维吾尔族长辫子 | 100 |
| 刺绣技艺·蒙古族 | 97 | 可依米塞克头饰 | 101 |

# Contents

Forward — Li Qinzeng

## Historic Architecture

| | |
|---|---|
| Dihua Town | 3 |
| Laoman Town · Dwelling House | 4 |
| Laoman Town · Drum Tower | 5 |
| Ancient Village Ruins · Main Entrance | 6 |
| Ancient Village Ruins · Alley | 7 |
| Six Star Street · Russian House | 8 |
| Six Star Street · Architectural Decoration | 9 |
| Lijie Street · Two-Story Building | 10 |
| Lijie Street · House Gate | 11 |
| Lijie Street · Street Corner | 12 |
| Lijie Street · Uygur Dwelling House | 13 |
| Lijie Street · Hui House | 14 |
| Lijie Street · Wusun Post Office | 15 |
| Hongshan Pagoda | 16 |
| Yili General's House | 17 |
| Shaanxi Hui Temple | 18 |
| Century-Old Seed Oil Mill | 19 |
| Ancient Town Cellar Wall in Qitai | 20 |
| Qitai Ancient Town Cellar · Wine Brewing Tools | 21 |
| Thalat Mazar | 22 |
| Pebble Tombs | 23 |
| Qiemuerqieke Cemetery | 24 |
| Adunqiaomu Stone Tomb | 25 |
| Kekeshemulaokemuqi Stone Statue | 26 |
| Stone Statues in Agung Getty Grassland | 27 |
| Kerangtuoluohai Stone Statue | 28 |

## Vernacular Architecture

| | |
|---|---|
| Uygur House · Architectural complex | 31 |
| Uygur House · Bungalow | 32 |
| Uygur House · Courtyard | 33 |
| Uygur House Doors | 34 |
| Outdoor Corridor | 35 |
| Grapevine Village | 36 |
| Raisin Drying Room · Panorama | 37 |
| Raisin Drying Room · Wall | 38 |
| Mosque Tower | 39 |
| Karez Well | 40 |
| Water Storage Dam | 41 |
| Yili River · Plank Road | 42 |
| Yili River · Wooden bridge | 43 |

| | |
|---|---|
| Daxigou · Wooden Plank Road | 44 |
| Kalajun Grassland · Dwelling | 45 |
| Winter Shelter · Panorama | 46 |
| Winter Shelter · Wall | 47 |
| Winter Shelter · Building Materials | 48 |
| Winter Shelter · Ruins | 49 |
| Kazak Village · Panorama | 50 |
| Kazak Village · Dwelling | 51 |
| Kazak Village · Stone Wall | 52 |
| Kazak Village · Fence | 53 |
| Kazak Village · Sheep Pen | 54 |
| Kazak Village · Barn | 55 |
| Kazak Yurt · Exterior | 56 |
| Kazak Yurt · Interior | 57 |
| Mongolian Camp · Panorama | 58 |
| Mongolian Camp · Yurt | 59 |
| Mongolian Camp · Hut | 60 |
| Mongolian Camp · Outdoor Kitchen | 61 |
| Tuwa Dwelling House · Village | 62 |
| Tuwa House · Architecture | 63 |
| Tuwa House · Yard | 64 |
| Low-Lying Hut · Close View | 65 |
| Low-Lying Hut · Door | 66 |
| Low-Lying Hut · Barrack | 67 |
| Rammed-Clay-Wall House | 68 |

## Folk Customs

| | |
|---|---|
| Bazaar | 71 |
| Bazaar | 72 |
| Cobblers | 73 |
| Blacksmith | 74 |
| Seasonal Transition Team | 75 |
| Seasonal Transition Herdsmen | 76 |
| Herdsmen and Horses | 77 |
| Teenagers on Horseback | 78 |
| Eagle Tamer | 79 |
| Woman Sieving Grain | 80 |
| Beekeepers | 81 |
| Bee Hive | 82 |
| Making Milk Wine | 83 |
| Making Milk Wine | 84 |
| People Filling Milk Wine | 85 |
| Oboo Ritual | 86 |
| Weddings | 87 |
| Meshrep | 88 |
| Challenging | 89 |

| | | | |
|---|---|---|---|
| Sheep-Fighting | 90 | Embroidery Skills · Kazak | 96 |
| Ritual Song | 91 | Embroidery Skills · Mongolian | 97 |
| Kuiyi | 92 | Palas Making Skill | 98 |
| Karajurha | 93 | Red Wicker Weaving Skills | 99 |
| Kazak Yurt Building Skills | 94 | Uygur Long Braids | 100 |
| Uygur Embroidery Skills | 95 | Keyimisek Headdress | 101 |

# 自 序

从自然地理上来说，天山将新疆分成南、北两部分，天山以北称为北疆，天山以南称为南疆。从文化地理上来说，丝绸之路进入新疆后分成三条支线，位于北疆的是丝绸之路的北道，这条支线又被称作"草原丝绸之路"；位于南疆的是丝绸之路的中道和南道，这两条支线又被称作"沙漠丝绸之路"或"绿洲丝绸之路"。"丝绸之路"不仅是一个文化象征符号，还是一个"历史上特殊的人文区域"。

"草原丝绸之路"又叫做"欧亚草原之路"或"毛皮之路"，东起东北的大兴安岭以至朝鲜半岛和日本，西可达俄罗斯的南西伯利亚和中亚的北部地区。这条道路曾是丝绸之路的主干道，至秦汉之后才逐渐成为辅路，它在欧亚经济贸易、文化交流中发挥着重要的作用。

匈奴、乌孙、鲜卑、突厥、蒙古等游牧民族是"草原丝绸之路"的开拓者和经营者，强势游牧民族的"草原军力"有效地保障了这条道路的通畅。汤因比认为草原像"未经耕种的海洋"一样，它虽然不能为定居的人类提供居住条件，但是却为旅行和运输提供了更大的方便。草原民族为东西方政治、经济、文化、语言的交流做出了重要的贡献。

与历史上"草原丝绸之路"兴盛时期相比，如今北疆地区的民族结构发生了很大的变化，他们和睦共处、竞相争艳、各显芬芳，为新疆的政治稳定、经济发展、文化繁荣做出了巨大的贡献。生活在这里的民族，既有居住在"移动的城堡"里，每年不断在"冬窝子"与"夏窝子"之间"转场"的哈萨克族人；也有历史上清政府收复伊犁后从阿克苏、乌什、拜城、库车、沙雅、喀什噶尔、叶尔羌、和田等南疆诸地移民过来的回族民众；既有随渥巴锡东归的蒙古族土尔扈特部、从东北盛京等十三城西迁过来的锡伯族；还有从黑龙江西迁过来的索伦人(鄂温克族)、达呼尔人(达斡尔族)和由热河、凉州、庄浪、西安迁移过来的满族人，从沙皇俄国南迁过来的俄罗斯族。居住在北疆的其他民族还有汉族、乌孜别克族、塔塔尔族、柯尔克孜族、塔吉克族等。

本书以生活在北疆地区各民族群众的居住空间为主线，以图文并茂的方式向读者介绍了各民族的精神信仰、日常生活与生产、传统技艺、传统乐舞与体育等领域的非物质文化形态。对于北疆地区浩如烟海的民族知识、地方性知识和生活经验来说，本书精心遴选的96幅图画犹如管中窥豹，无法帮助读者确立对于北疆自然地理、人文风情、文化形态的相对系统的知识体系，惟希望读者借此图画打开理解北疆的过去、现在及未来发展的一扇窗户。最后，对学苑出版社洪文雄为本书的出版事宜所提供的建议与帮助深表感谢。

# Forward

In terms of natural geography, the Tianshan Mountains divide Xinjiang into Southern Xinjiang and Northern Xinjiang. From the perspective of cultural geography, the Silk Road in Xinjiang developed into three branches: north Silk Road located in Northern Xinjiang, known as the "Prairie Silk Road"; the middle and south roads located in Southern Xinjiang, were known respectively as "Desert Silk Road" and "Oasis Silk Road".

More than just a cultural symbol, the "Silk Road" was a "special habitat in human history". Before the "Desert Silk Road" became famous, the "Prairie Silk Road" was the main route, but after the Qin and Han dynasties (221B.C.-220A.D.), it gradually became the auxiliary route of the "Desert Silk Road", playing an important role in the economy, trade, and cultural exchange between Europe and Asia.

Nomadic people were the pioneers and primary users of the "Prairie Silk Road", with a strong army to safeguard it. Prairie nomads played an important role in the exchange of politics, economy, culture and language between the East and the West.

Today, the ethnic makeup of the Northern region has greatly changed. The people have made great contributions to the national security, political stability, economic development and cultural prosperity of Xinjiang in a harmonious way. Ethnic groups living here include Kazakh, Uygur, Mongolian, Xibo, Ewenki, Daur, Manchu, Russian, Han, Hui, Uzbek, Tatar, Kirgiz, Tajik.

This book portrays the living space of all ethnic groups in the northern region, complemented by text and sketchs showing the spiritual beliefs, daily life, production, traditional skills, traditional music and dance, sports and other non-material cultural forms. Readers will be delighted to learn the past, present and future trends of Northern Xinjiang portrayed in this book. Special gratitude goes to Hong Wenxiong of the Academy Press for his assistance in preparing this book.

Li Qinzeng

# 历史建筑
Historic Architecture

迪化城

位于乌鲁木齐市内，始建于清乾隆三十一年（1766年）。"迪化"为"启迪教化"之意，是乌鲁木齐的旧称。该城周长约8000米，设有七座城门，包含正门四座，分别为东门（惠孚门）、南门（肇阜门）、西门（丰庆门）、北门（景惠门）；偏门三座，分别为小南门、小东门、小西门。图为迪化城城楼。

### Dihua Town

Built in 1766, in Urumqi City, "Dihua", the old name of Urumqi, means "enlightenment". The town is about 8 km long, with seven gates-4 main and 3 side ones. The sketch shows the Tower of Dihua Town.

老满城·民居

老满城古称"巩宁城",位于乌鲁木齐市内,在迪化城旁。始建于清乾隆三十八年(1773年),曾是一座满族驻防城。城内既有炮楼、箭楼、兵房、正城楼、瓮城楼、角楼、堆房、仓库、鼓楼等军事设施,还有乌鲁木齐都统、知州、领队大臣等衙署设施,以及关帝庙、城隍庙、文昌宫等庙宇祠堂。图为老满城民居。

**Laoman Town · Dwelling House**
Built in 1773, located in Urumqi City, it has military and office facilities, temples and an ancestral hall. The sketch shows the dwelling house of Laoman Town.

### 老满城·鼓楼

位于老满城的中心，始建于乾隆三十八年（1773年）。老满城古称"巩宁"，取"巩固安宁"之意，鼓楼按照都城的形制，建在城市的中央。其西是乌鲁木齐都统署，其南是领队大臣衙署，其东是镇迪道衙署，其北是家眷住房。学校、磨坊、养济院、城隍庙、文昌宫、关帝庙都分布在其周围。图为老满城的鼓楼。

### Laoman Town · Drum Tower

Built in 1773, it is in the center of Laoman Town, with the Urumqi government to the west, military headquarters to the south, the local government office mansion to the east, and family housing to the north. Schools, mills, Chenghuang Temple and other structures are located here. The sketch shows the Laoman Drum Tower.

> 亚尔果勒村·正门

  位于吐鲁番市亚尔乡的亚尔果勒村，毗邻交河故城，已有数百年的历史。为维吾尔族古村落，现该村落占地二万余平方米，内部设有多功能生态广场，维吾尔民俗陈列馆和传统民居展示区。是一处全面展示维吾尔原生态民俗风情和交河历史文化底蕴的旅游景区。图为古村落遗迹的正门。

**Ancient Village Ruins · Main Entrance**
Hundreds of years old, Yar Guole Village of Turpan City is adjacent to ancient Jiaohe city. This old Uygur village covers an area of 20,000 square meters. The sketch shows the village's main entrance.

| 亚尔果勒村·小巷 |

　　村落中的民居用生黄土砖坯建造，墙皮也是用黄泥抹的，墙砖上砌有花纹。建筑多为院落式，房屋呈正方形，留有伊斯兰风格的小尖顶。前廊较深，庭院中栽种花卉、葡萄，还有专门用来晾晒葡萄干的晾房。图为古村落中的小巷。

### Ancient Village Ruins · Alley

The houses in the ancient villages were constructed of loess brick. Most are of the square, courtyard style; small Islamic style spires still remain. The sketch shows a village alley.

**六星街·俄式民居**

　　位于伊宁市内,始建于1934年,是一处集中展示俄罗斯族传统文化的历史街区。几十年前,这里的俄罗斯居民占居民总数的60%,后大部分侨民逐渐离开。目前这里居住着维吾尔族、俄罗斯族、塔塔尔族等少数民族。这里的俄罗斯特色建筑都得到了很好的保存。图为六星街的一处俄罗斯式样的民居。

**Six Star Street · Russian House**
Founded in 1934 in Yining City, it is a historic district reflecting Russian traditional culture in its well-preserved Russian architecture. The sketch is of a Russian house on Six Star Street.

**六星街·装饰局部**

六星街的设计规划由德国工程师瓦斯里完成,原名"六政街",取自民国时期新疆省政府推行的"反帝、反苏、民族平等、和平、建设、清廉"六大政策之意。目前六星街是伊宁市重要的历史旅游景区和特色商业区。图为六星街上一处建筑装饰的局部。

**Six Star Street · Architectural Decoration**
Formerly known as "Six Policies Street", its name refers to the implementation of the six provincial government policies of the Republic of China (1912-1949). Currently, Six Star Street is an important cultural tourism site in Yining, a leisure area and characteristic business district. The sketch shows details of the architectural decoration.

离街·二层小楼

位于伊犁哈萨克自治州特克斯县城内,博斯坦街南端,始建于1936年。特克斯县城因八卦布局而闻名,是世界上最大、保存最完整的八卦城。城市整体呈放射状圆形,街道网状分布,路路相通、街街相连。"离街"的名称取自八卦中的"离卦"。图为离街中的一座二层的民族风格的建筑。

## Lijie Street · Two-Story Building

This street was developed in 1936 in Turks County of the Kazak Autonomous Prefecture in Yili. Turks County is famous for its Eight Diagrams layout, the largest and best preserved example in the world. The sketch shows a two-story Kazak style building on Lijie Street.

离街·宅院大门

　　离街于2016年6月扩建完工，街道有两条，呈"U"型分布，汇集了老特克斯县城的历史记忆和乡愁，是一个集民居建筑、民族风情、民宿体验、民族工艺品、民族美食、休闲服务为一体的综合文化街区。每到夜晚，在离街前的小广场上，特克斯镇各社区草根艺人纷纷登台献艺。图为离街一处宅院大门。

**Lijie Street · House Gate**

The expansion project of Lijie Street was completed in June 2016. With two routes forming a "U", the street serves as an integrated cultural district displaying houses, ethnic customs, guest experience opportunities, national handicrafts and national cuisine. The sketch shows a house gate.

**离街·街角**

　　离街住有居民42户，有哈萨克族、汉族、回族、维吾尔族、蒙古族、柯尔克孜族等。街区总长610米，总面积约2.5万平方米，32座院落各具特色。图为离街的一个街角。

### Lijie Street · Street Corner
This block has 42 households composed of six ethnic groups. The street is 610 meters long with an area of 25,000 square meters and 32 distinctive courtyards.

| 离街·维吾尔族民居 |

  离街集中展示了哈萨克族、维吾尔族、蒙古族、汉族、回族、柯尔克孜族等民族的文化元素，民居院落既有维吾尔族雕刻的铁皮大门、木门、瓷砖拼贴画，又有图瓦人用圆木垒砌的院墙和木屋，还有回族的雕窗、雕花围墙等建筑或装饰样式。图为离街的一所维吾尔族民居。

## Lijie Street · Uygur Dwelling House
Lijie Street shows cultural elements of various ethnic groups in Xinjiang. Its 32 residential courtyards have Uygur doors, Tuva walls and huts, Hui carved windows and other architectural, decorative styles.

**离街·回族民居**

　　离街两侧房屋的墙面上，均有反映少数民族生活的绘画或浮雕；离街的房屋也保留了各少数民族独特的风格。图为离街的一所回族民居。

## Lijie Street · Hui House

Protecting the diversity of traditional culture, the house walls feature the paintings and reliefs depicting the life of ethnic minorities; the houses here also retain the unique ethnic styles. The sketch shows a Hui house on Lijie Street.

离街·乌孙邮局

图为离街的乌孙邮局。

**Lijie Street · Wusun Post Office**

Lijie Street is an example of the transformation of the old city, retaining the traditional street layout while adding modern tourism services and functions. The sketch shows the Wusun post office.

红山宝塔

又名"镇龙宝塔",位于乌鲁木齐市区中心,乌鲁木齐河东岸,红山的最高处,始建于清乾隆五十三年(1788年)。红山以其西端断崖呈褐红色得名,古人称其为"神山"。宝塔高10.6米,为六面九级八角顶的青砖实心塔。"塔映夕阳"是乌鲁木齐老八景中的一个奇观。

## Hongshan Pagoda
Built in 1788 in the center of Urumqi on the east bank of the Urumqi River and on the highest point of Hongshan, the six-sided, nine-story brick pagoda with an octagonal roof is 10.6 meters high.

### 伊犁将军府

位于霍城县惠远乡惠远古城中心,始建于清光绪八年(1882年)。将军府坐北朝南,整个建筑为四合院式,主要建筑有军府大门、将军府正殿、将军亭、东西营房、客房、书房等。图为伊犁将军府钟鼓楼。

### Yili General's House

Founded in 1882, in ancient Huiyuan city center of Huiyuan Township in Huocheng County, the south-facing buildings include the gate, main hall, general's quarters, east and west barracks, guest rooms, sludy, etc. The sketch shows the house bell tower.

### 陕西回族大寺

原名"宁固寺",又名"凤凰寺""金顶寺""陕西大寺""陕甘大寺"。位于伊宁市汉人街,始建于清乾隆二十五年(1760年)。该寺仿照陕西省西安市化觉巷清真寺修建,采用中国传统建筑工艺,兼有阿拉伯伊斯兰风格。寺院以礼拜殿为主体建筑,分外殿、中殿、里殿。殿前后、两侧分别有卷棚、走廊。

### Shaanxi Hui Temple

Also known as Ninggu Temple, Phoenix Temple, Jinding Temple, Shaanxi Temple and Shaanxi and Gansu Temple, it is located on Han Street in Yining City. Built in 1760, the temple features traditional Chinese and Arabic Islam architectural styles.

> 老油坊

    位于巴里坤哈萨克自治县大河镇，始建于19世纪40年代，是新疆迄今保存最完好的杠杆式榨油作坊之一。传统的榨油方法是，先将油料放进炒锅，用微火炒至微糊，再把炒好的油料用畜力牵引的石磨磨成浆后，放进木制的蒸笼里蒸，待满屋蒸汽升腾时，凭人力拉动油梁挤压出油。图为用青石凿成的磨盘。

### Century-Old Seed Oil Mill

Founded in the 1940s, in Dahe town of Barkol Kazak Autonomous County, it is Xinjiang's best-preserved seed oil press workshop. The traditional method of oil extraction is: fry the oil seeds in a wok over a gentle fire until lightly browned, then grind the oil seeds into a pulp using the animal-powered stone mill, then put the pulp into a wooden steamer; lastly, use the press beam to squeeze out the oil. The sketch shows the chiseled bluestone mill.

**奇台古城窖·墙面**

　　位于奇台县,始建于18世纪中叶,号称为"新疆第一窖"。古窖址仅存一面砖墙,由青砖垒砌而成,墙面涂有一层白灰。全长11.8米,高2.1米,分为两部分。北面部分每隔1.2米有固定木板的插槽,两侧墙体上有供人攀爬的脚窝。南面部分墙面有两处隔墙残迹,为发酵池隔墙。图为古城窖遗址墙面。

**Ancient Town Cellar Wall in Qitai**

Built in the mid-18th Century, and known as the "First Cellar in Xinjiang", it is in the Ancient Town Wine Company of Qitai County. All that remains of the site is one section of the black brick wall coated with a layer of gray.

奇台古城窖·酿酒工具

关于奇台酿酒技艺的记载，最早的始自明代陈诚所著的《西域蕃国志》。明代末年，大量汉族人来到新疆，奇台窖酒酿造技艺兴起。至清光绪年间（1871～1908年），奇台山西巷的酒坊已达13家，其品质尤以"杏林坊"最佳，其核心技艺是"水甘、料实、工精、器洁、曲时、窖湿"。图为现在使用的酿酒工具。

**Qitai Ancient Town Cellar · Wine Brewing Tools**
During the late Ming Dynasty (1368-1644), with many Han people coming to Xinjiang, wine brewing technology developed in Qitai up until reign of Qing Emperor Guangxu (1871-1908). In Shanxi Lane, there were 13 distilleries, among which "Xinglin Distillery" boasted the best quality. The sketch shows the wine brewing tools.

### 塔尔阿特麻扎

位于伊吾县千山哈萨克自治乡驻地西部山中,距离县城130千米。维吾尔语意为"马脊形山坡上的墓地",伊斯兰教传教士塔尔阿特葬于此。该麻扎为庭院式建筑,依山而建,包括大门、木栅栏围墙、主墓室以及为牧民礼拜而修建的房屋等。

### Thalat Mazar

Built during the period from 1882 to 1930, it is in the western mountains of Qianshan Kazak Autonomous County 130 km from Yiwu county. Islam missionary Thalat is buried here. The mazar is a courtyard-style structure which includes gates, wooden fence, tombs and houses of worship.

### 卵石墓

位于塔城市区的西北角，乌拉斯台河东西两岸的二级台地上，为公元前1000年前的文化遗存。共有墓葬19座，分有巨石砌成的石棺墓和卵石砌成的石室墓两种。卵石墓属石室墓，分熨斗形、椭圆形、圆形三种；葬法分火葬和侧身屈肢葬两种。该图的墓葬形制为熨斗形屈肢葬。

### Pebble Tombs

These 1000-year cultural relics are in the northwest corner of Tacheng, on the city's medical school campus both sides of the Ulasi River. The 19 Pebble Tombs are iron-shaped stone chambers.

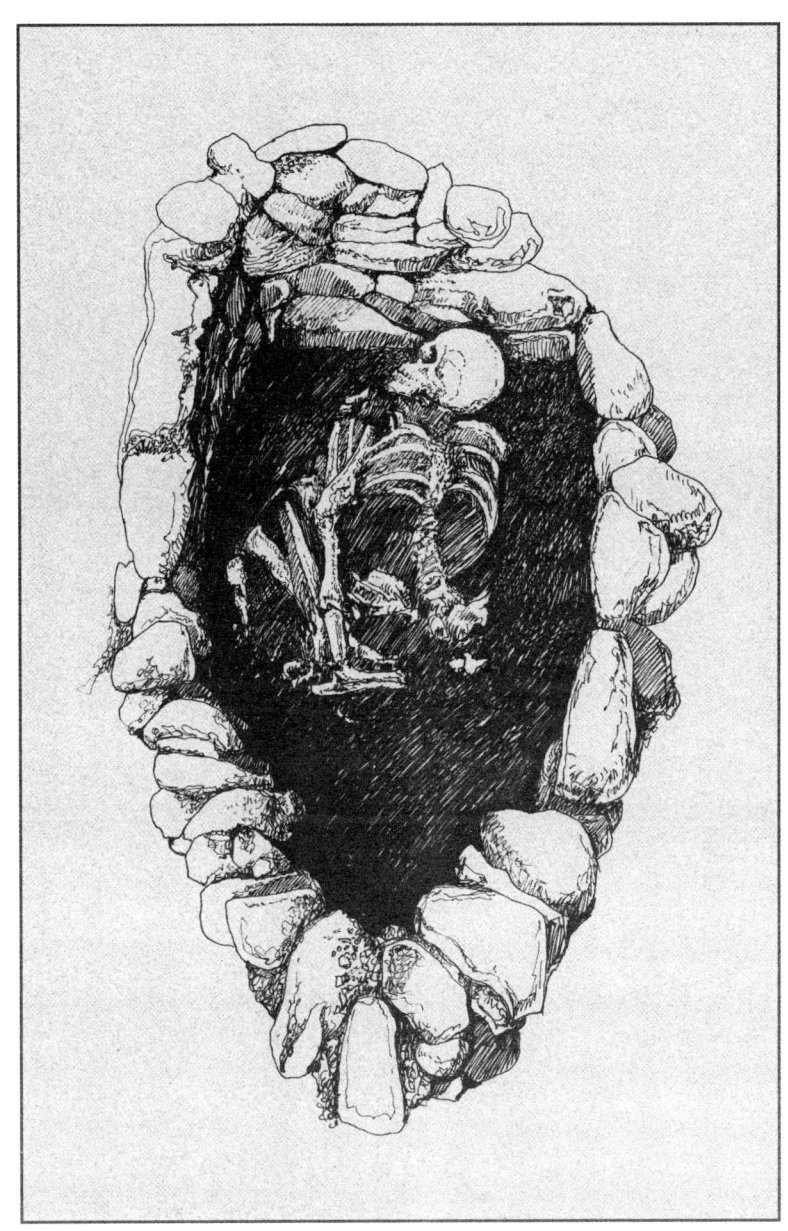

23

## 切木尔切克墓地

位于阿勒泰市西南12千米的山间盆地中,葬的时间墓从公元前1000年一直延续到10世纪的隋唐时期,考古上称其为"切木尔切克文化"。墓葬形制有石人石堆墓、石围石棺墓、石棺石人墓等,出土有石器、陶器、铜器、铁器、骨器等物。图为其中的喀依纳尔一号墓地石人。

### Qiemuerqieke Cemetery

Located in the basin 12 km southwest of Altay Town, the cemetery dates from the Bronze Age (1000 BC) to the Sui and Tang Dynasties (581-907), and is archaeologically called "Qiemuerqieke culture." The sketch shows the stone statue on tomb No.1.

### 阿敦乔鲁石堆墓

　　位于博尔塔拉蒙古自治州温泉县西北阿拉套山南麓的草原上，阿敦乔鲁遗址区南部。19~公元前17世纪，为青铜时代早期的墓葬。"阿敦乔鲁"为蒙古语，意为"像马群一样的石头"。墓葬的形制基本为方形石围、石棺墓。该石围栏墓由大量石板组成，呈方形，边长9.5米，最大石板的面积达3.25平方米。

### Adunqiaomu Stone Tomb

Located in the southern grassland of Dzungarian Alatau Mountain southwest of Hot Spring County in the Mongolian Autonomous Prefecture of Bortala, the tomb dates from the early Bronze Age-19th to the 17th century B.C.. Its slate stone fence forms a square, each side of which is 9.5 meters long, the largest slate stone being 3.25 square meters.

## 科克舍木老克木齐石人

位于阿勒泰市区西南12千米处切木尔切克石人墓附近的戈壁上,为公元前5～公元前2世纪的遗物。石人为女性石雕,通高1.1米,露出地面高75厘米,宽80厘米。刻石为没有经加工的砾石,浮雕出人脸和手臂,面廓以边框形式的浮起,五官用浮雕表现,阴刻弧形嘴,两臂屈于胸前,作抚状,胸前有连弧形饰。

**Kekeshemulaokemuqi Stone Statue**

Located in the Gobi Desert 12 km southwest of Altay town, it dates from the 15th to the 2nd Century B.C. The statue is of a woman, 1.1 meters high, 0.8 meters wide, set 0.75 meters above the ground.

### 阿贡盖提草原石人阵

位于阿勒泰地区布尔津县城至喀纳斯风景旅游区96千米公路旁,年代可追溯到2600多年前。"阿贡盖提"为蒙古语,是"阳光普照的地方"的意思,阿贡盖提草原是阿勒泰地区哈萨克等游牧民族的发祥地之一,也是布尔津县古代文明的摇篮之一。该处有17座石人,图为其中的一座。

**Stone Statues in Agung Getty Grassland**

Built more than 2,600 years ago, the 17 stone statues of human figures are next to the 96th km site along the road between Burqin county and Kanas scenic tourist area in Altay Town. The sketch shows one of the 17 stone statues of human figures.

## 喀让格托海石人

位于阿勒泰地区青河县大青格里河中游西岸谷地上的喀让格托海墓地中，约为公元前7～2世纪的铁器时代早期遗物。石人高1.17米，宽0.4米。刻石为长方形花岗岩石板，仅雕刻面孔和衣领，脸呈椭圆形，以浮雕表现五官。弧形眉，嘴微宽，略呈噘状。下额凸出且圆，阴刻出额部，衣领为双翻领。

### Kerangtuoluohai Stone Statue

Located in front of the stone tomb on the west bank of the middle Daqing Gerry River of Qinghe County in Altay town, the relic dates from the seventh century B.C. to the second century A.D. It is 1.17 meters high and 0.4 meters wide.

# 乡土建筑
Vernacular Architecture

### 维吾尔族民居·建筑群

  吐鲁番地区夏季酷热、冬天酷寒，风沙大。维吾尔族人创造性地发明了包含半地下室或地下室的平顶建筑形制。同时，为了采光，有的在屋顶上开设天窗，室内砌土炕，有的土炕大得占有半间屋的面积。于此，民居的地下部分夏季凉爽宜人，冬季则温暖舒适。

### Uygur House · Architectural complex

In sandy Turpan, the weather is hot in summer and cold in winter. The Uygur people invented a flat-top building with a skylight, a semi-basement or basement, and a heated sleeping platform indoor. The house is warm in winter and cool in summer. The sketch shows a typical Uygur house architecture.

> 维吾尔族民居·平房

  吐鲁番地区的维吾尔族民居深受中亚地区流行的平顶建筑的影响，墙壁多以生土夯筑而成，房前有较深的带护栏的围廊。庭院中多种植果树、葡萄、花卉等植物，是休息、餐饮、弹唱之所。

**Uygur House · Bungalow**
In Turpan, Uygur house walls are mostly made of rammed loess, and the porch are fence surrounded. Bedecked with varieties of plants, the courtyard is used for relaxation, dining, play and singing. The sketch shows a typical Uygur bungalow.

维吾尔族民居·院落

在伊宁市,传统的维吾尔族院落里一般都有白杨树、葡萄架、花圃和茶棚。葡萄架下是室外聚会、休闲娱乐的地方,花圃则给整个院子带来蓬勃生气,茶棚或葡萄架下是歇凉之地,也是妇女们制作传统食品的地方。

**Uygur House · Courtyard**

In Yining, the traditional Uygur courtyard has poplar trees, grapevines, a flower garden and a tea shed. The grapevines shade outdoor parties and the tea shed is a cool place to prepare traditional food. The sketch shows a typical Uygur courtyard.

| 维吾尔族民居·大门 |

　　伊宁的维吾尔族民居大门以木雕、面砖装饰和彩绘为主要装饰手段，其装饰图案反映出吐鲁番地区多元文化融合的特点。门一般为木制，其上有看叶、门钉、门板、铺手和门扣环，门板上一般镶嵌着用铁皮雕刻的几何或花卉图案。在雕法上有线雕、浅浮雕及透雕等。

## Uygur House Doors

Yining, Uygur house doors are usually wooden, with decorative leaves, door nails, panels, handles and door rings. Doors are usually inlaid with carved metal of geometric or floral patterns. This sketch shows a typical Uygur house door.

### 维吾尔族民居·檐廊

伊宁市维吾尔族的典型建筑形式。外廊又叫做"檐廊"。檐廊与檐等高,讲究的民居还有柱子与檐相接。柱面多为四、六、八、十二边,同一根柱子通过变化柱面来形成装饰。从空间分割上来说,檐廊是室内活动与室外活动之间的过渡地带;从功能上来说,檐廊是进行诸多民俗活动的重要文化空间。

### Outdoor Corridor

The building is a typical Uygur architectural form in Yining. The outdoor corridor is called an "eaves corridor". The cylindrical surfaces of four, six, eight or twelve ridges form decorative planes on the pillars.

### 葡萄沟

　　位于吐鲁番市区东北约11千米的葡萄沟，海拔300米左右，南北长约8000米，东西宽约2000米，是火焰山下的一处峡谷。沟内有布依鲁克河流过，其主要水源为高山融雪，因盛产葡萄而得名，是吐鲁番地区的著名旅游胜地。

### Grapevine Village

Located in the Grape Valley Township at the foot of Flaming Mountain about 11 km northwest of Turpan City, the village is 300 meters above sea level, about 8 km from north to south end, and 2 km from east to west. The valley here is known for its rich grapes.

葡萄干晾房·全景

晾房一般为生土建筑，根据其存在位置大致分成两种类型。一种位于山坡荒地上，被称作独立式葡萄晾房；一种修建于自家住房顶上，被称作居家葡萄晾房。图为独立式葡萄干晾房。

**Raisin Drying Room · Panorama**

Generally built of loess, drying rooms are of two types according to location. One stands on the hillside wasteland, known as the independent raisin drying room; the other is built on top of its owner's house and known as the home raisin drying room. The sketch shows a typical raisin drying room.

葡萄干晾房·墙体

　　晾房一般建在通风情况比较好的地方，分为上下两层。上层房子用土坯砖块垒成，墙上留有很多通风用的孔道。果农将新鲜葡萄挂在上层，利用自然风将葡萄晾干。下层多用来居住或存放东西。图为葡萄干晾房的墙体。

### Raisin Drying Room · Wall

Drying rooms have two levels. There are a lot of ventilation holes in the wall of the upper level. The growers hang the fresh grapes on the upper level and allow the natural wind to dry them. The lower level serves as a living room or storage room. The sketch shows the wall of a drying room.

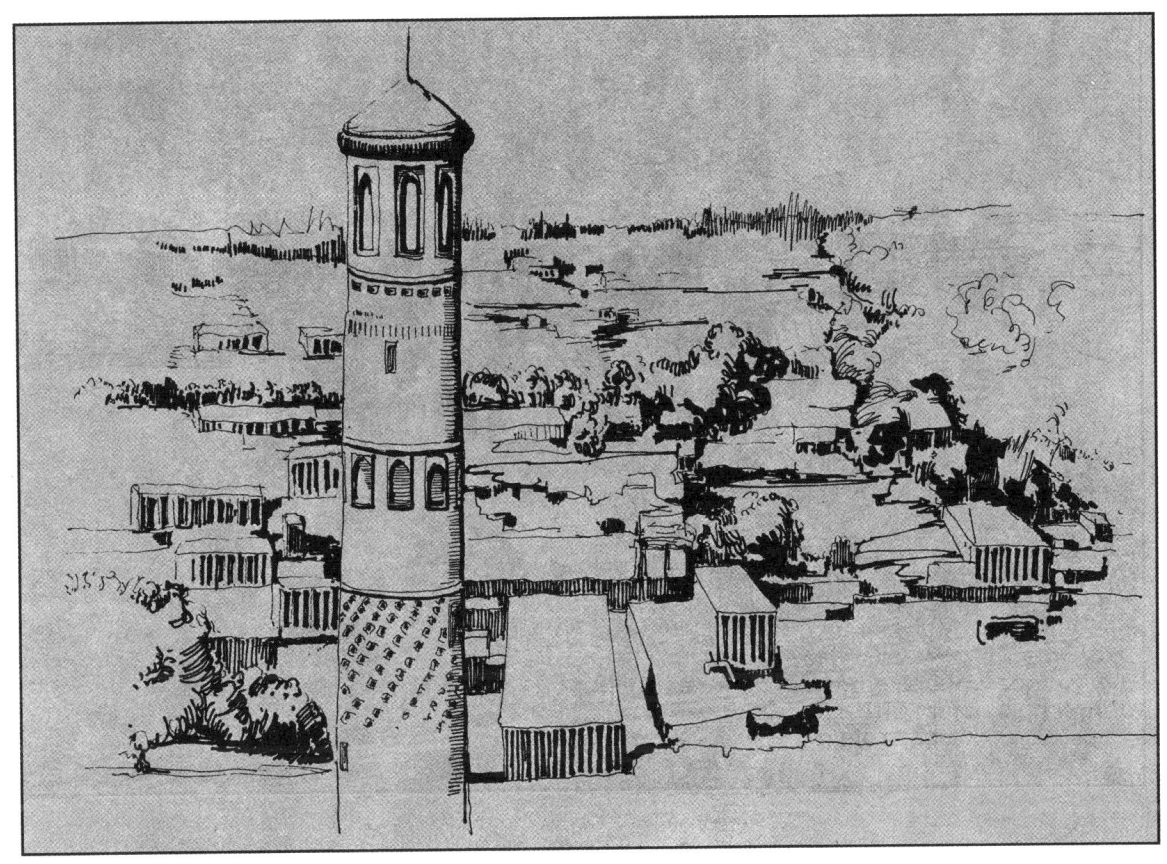

> 清真寺塔楼

  在新疆农村，信奉伊斯兰民众较集中的村庄一般会有一座清真寺，人口数量较少的则几个村庄联合修建一座清真寺。他们把每个星期五称作"主麻日"，每天正午他们要去清真寺参加集体礼拜。图为吐鲁番某清真寺塔楼。

## Mosque Tower

In Xinjiang rural areas, there are usually mosques in villages where Islamic people live. Muslims go to the mosques at noon every Friday to worship. This sketch shows the mosque tower in Turpan.

### 坎儿井

　　汉语文献称为"井渠",维吾尔语称之为"坎儿孜"。坎儿井普遍存在于吐鲁番和哈密地区,是干旱地区绿洲农业中的一种独特的水利灌溉工程。从结构上来说,坎儿井主要由竖井、暗渠、明渠、涝坝四部分组成。

### Karez Well

Prevalent in the Turpan and Hami areas, this is a unique water irrigation project for oasis agriculture in arid areas. The well structure is composed of shaft, culvert, open channel, and water storage dam.

### 涝坝

  维吾尔语称作"库勒",是新疆干旱地区为满足村民的生活用水而开挖的一种露天的水塘,是维吾尔族绿洲生活的重要文化意象。涝坝是村落的重要公共文化活动空间,其附近一般建有清真寺。本图为伊犁河边的一处涝坝旅游景观。

### Water Storage Dam
This open-air pond stores essential water for villagers in arid areas of Xinjiang. These dams, generally with mosques nearby, are important places for village cultural activities. This is a sketch of a typical dam by the Yili River.

伊犁河·栈道

　　伊犁河古称"亦列水""伊丽水"。汉武帝称伊犁河为"神的特殊恩赐"。此外，伊犁河谷还被称作"中亚人种博物馆"和"生物天堂"，是全球水、土、光、热合理组合的地区之一。图为伊犁河上修建的栈道。

## Yili River · Plank Road

Han Emperor Wu Di (147-87 B.C.) called the Yili River a "special gift of God". It is also known as the "Central Ethnic Museum" and "Biological Paradise", which is a natural combination of water, soil, light and heat. This sketch shows a plank road built over the Yili River.

伊犁河·木桥

　　伊犁河河谷是丝绸之路北道上非常重要的文明通道和军事要塞，这里是清代新疆地区最高军政长官——伊犁将军的驻地。除了汉族之外，这里曾经生活过大月氏人、乌孙人、匈奴人、突厥人、蒙古人、维吾尔人等民族。图为伊犁河上的一座木桥。

**Yili River · Wooden bridge**
As the site of the residence of the military governor (a general) of Xinjiang during the Qing Dynasty (1644-1911), the Yili River Valley is a very important cultural location and military fortress along the North Silk Road. The sketch shows a wooden bridge over the Yili River.

### 大西沟

　　大西沟距离霍城县城50千米左右为一条野果沟，沟内生长着60多种野果，是伊犁河河谷"生物天堂"的重要组成部分。图为大西沟景区的一条木栈道。

**Daxigou · Wooden Plank Road**

Daxigou is about 50km from Huocheng County, known for Daxigou Valley and Daxigou River. The sketch shows a wooden plank road in Daxigou.

喀拉峻草原

　　哈萨克族牧民过着"逐水草而居"的生活，由于草场资源的承载力有限以及天气变化等方面的原因，牧民不得不从一个草场转移到另一个草场。春季转场的时间一般在4月份，秋季转场的时间一般在9月份。喀拉峻草原优质牧草有上百种，是特克斯县、巩留县哈萨克族牧民的夏牧场。图为喀拉峻草原上的民居。

**Kalajun Grassland · Dwelling**
Kazak herdsmen must move from pasture to pasture due to limited capacity of the pastures and the seasonal weather changes. Spring transition time is April, and autumn transition time is September. Karajun grassland is the summer pasture of the Kazak herdsmen of Tekes and Gongliu Counties. The sketch shows houses on the Kalajun grassland.

冬窝子·全景

又叫"冬牧场",是哈萨克族牧人过冬的地方。一般建在具有环形山谷、山坳或盆地等能有效躲避暴风雪的地势中。毡房以四块房墙为最多,一个小家庭,有四块房墙就够用。经济条件好的人家多住八块或八块以上房墙构成的毡房。图为某冬窝子全景。

**Winter Shelter · Panorama**
This is the type of place where the Kazaks and their livestock stay in winter. Winter shelter is generally built at in valleys, gullies or basins where they can shelter from storms. The sketch shows the panorama of a winter shelter.

[冬窝子·墙面]

　　冬窝子的建筑材料一般为当地容易获得的溪流中的卵石、山石或土坯，牧民为了御寒保暖会在石头间隙填充羊粪，在房间里打造土炕，炕上铺上厚厚的羊毛毡，火炉燃烧羊粪来取暖，即使如此室内温度最冷也有可能达到零下30度。图为冬窝子的墙面。

Winter Shelter · Wall
Winter shelter building materials are generally stones or adobe; herdsmen use sheep manure to fill gaps between the stones to keep the warm air in and build heated sleeping platform covered with thick wool felt. The sketch shows a winter shelter wall.

冬窝子·转场

　　最近几年，牧民开始使用机械化设备来转场，一户牧民连同所有家当和牲畜，用汽车或拖拉机运送。原先需要五六天乃至一二十天的路程现在一天之内就可以完成。近年不断修建的牧道，也为转场提供了极大的方便。

Winter Shelter · Building Materials

In recent years, herders have begun using mechanized vehicles for transitions; their families and all their possessions and livestock are now transported by truck on government built roads for their convenience. The sketch shows building materials for winter shelters.

### 冬窝子·废墟

　　驱赶牲畜到冬窝子的工作一般由青壮年来完成，老年人和孩子一般住在定居点。每年10月底，哈萨克族牧民及其牲畜会入住冬窝子，一般会在此储存大量的草料。次年3月，哈萨克人便会驱赶牲畜从冬窝子离开，踏上转场之旅，最后到达夏牧场。图为牧民转场后的某冬窝子的废墟。

### Winter Shelter · Ruins
At the end of October, Kazak herdsmen and their livestock move to winter shelters. In March, they drive the livestock out of the winter shelter. The sketch shows the ruins of a winter shelter.

哈萨克族村庄·全景

从20世纪80年代起，国家启动了面向哈萨克族的退耕还草、牧民安居工程，在大的牧民安居点或者几个小安居点的基础上修建了学校、卫生所、体育运动场、图书室、市场等公共实施。图为某哈萨克族村庄的全景。

## Kazak Village · Panorama

In the 1980s, the government began a settlement project for Kazak herdsmen. These settlements have schools, health clinics, sports and other infrastructures. The sketch shows a panorama of such a Kazak village.

### 哈萨克族村庄·民居

　　哈萨克族村庄是哈萨克族定居的产物。定居房采用前有院后有圈的形式，一般会建有牛圈、羊圈，还会有拖拉机、摩托车等现代化的设施。定居后的哈萨克族牧民除了放牧外，还从事一部分农业或者手工业的生产。图为某哈萨克族村庄的民居。

### Kazak Village · Dwelling
A Kazak village is an important symbol of the modernization of Kazak. Settlement houses include cattle and sheep pens, and are equipped with tractors, motorcycles and other modern facilities. The sketch shows a Kazak village dwelling.

哈萨克族村庄·石头墙

　　哈萨克族仿照汉族、维吾尔族等农耕民族的建筑样式修建定居后的居所，邻里之间由院墙相隔。一般都有独立的院落，建筑材料多使用当地常见易得的石块、泥、木等材料。图为某哈萨克族村庄的石头墙。

**Kazak Village · Stone Wall**
Dwellings in Kazak villages generally have independent courtyards separated by walls built of stone, mud, or wood readily available. The sketch shows a Kazak village stone wall.

哈萨克族村庄·栅栏

在政府的引导和安置下，哈萨克族牧民脱离了单一的牧业生产方式，学习接受现代生产技术，通过发展家庭种养植业、创办民族手工业、投身旅游服务、进城务工等方式，形成了农牧商并举的生产经营模式，走上了家庭多元化创业发展的道路。图为某哈萨克族村庄的栅栏。

Kazak Village · Fence
Having changed the single production method of animal husbandry, Kazak herdsmen are learning modern production technology to diversify family enterprises. The sketch shows a typical Kazak village fence.

哈萨克族村庄·羊圈

哈萨克族传统的牧养方式以放养为主，定居后温暖的季节放牧，冬天在羊圈中饲养。同时，牧民开始运用现代的医疗技术，给牲畜注射疫苗，保持牲畜清洁，改良牲畜品种。图为某哈萨克族村庄的羊圈。

## Kazak Village · Sheep Pen

Kazak traditional pastoral way of raising livestock is grazing in the warm season and rearing them in winter pens. The sketch shows a Kazak village sheep pen.

{ 哈萨克族村庄·牲口棚 }

　　哈萨克族牧民在每年的12月至次年的3月间生活在村庄中，其他时间一般在牧场。定居后，夏秋季牧民会准备牲畜过冬的草料，囤积起来以备过冬所需。图为某哈萨克族村庄的牲口棚。

### Kazak Village · Barn
Kazak herdsmen live in villages from December to March and in pastures in the other months. In summer and autumn, they store livestock forage for the winter. The sketch shows a Kazak village barn.

哈萨克族毡房·外景

毡房的外面有供牲畜歇息的临时圈栏、栓马桩、炊灶等。为了保证视线的畅通，栓马桩一般位于毡房的后右方。炊灶一般距离毡房七八米远，炊灶旁的小棚子被称作"欧热叶"。图为某哈萨克族毡房外景。

**Kazak Yurt · Exterior**
There is a temporary fence for the livestock, a pile of firewood and a stove outside of the yurt. The hitching post is usually located at the rear right of the yurt. The cooking stove is generally seven or eight meters from the yurt. The sketch shows the yurt exterior Kazak yurt.

哈萨克族毡房·内景

父母的毡房叫做"大尚尔阿克",迎娶新娘的毡房叫做"奥塔吾",一般"奥塔吾"依附于"大尚尔阿克"而存在。毡房的主要功能是起居之用,为哈萨克族牧民待客、吃饭、休息、睡觉、做家务以及存储物品提供空间或场所。图为某哈萨克族毡房的内景。

### Kazak Yurt · Interior
Yurts provide a place for the Kazak herdsmen to prepare food, eat, rest, sleep, do housework and store items. The sketch shows a Kazak yurt interior.

蒙古族营地·全景

　　蒙古包冬季搭建在向阳背坡处，以避风雪；夏季则搭建在视野开阔、凉爽通风处，以防暑热。蒙古包外围春冬用毡子，而夏秋就因地而异多用草覆盖。图为东喀拉峻草原上牧人转场时所搭建的小蒙古包营地。

## Mongolian Camp · Panorama

In winter, yurts are built on sunny slopes to avoid snow. In summer, they are built in cool, well-ventilated place with good view. The sketch shows the panorama of a Mongolian grassland camp of small yurts built by the shepherd on the East Krakow grassland.

### 蒙古族营地·蒙古包

　　蒙古包是游牧时代蒙古族人的主要居住空间。蒙古包的形状和结构既是技术的选择，也是文化的选择。游牧民族生活在一望无际的茫茫草原上，极易产生"天圆地方"的想法。这种观念反映在民居上，就形成了围墙和天窗的圆形结构。图为某蒙古族营地的蒙古包。

**Mongolian Camp · Yurt**

The shape and structure of yurts is a choice of both technology and cultural. The square enclosure and the circular skylight reflects the concept of "round sky and square earth". The sketch shows yurts of a Mongolian camp.

蒙古族营地·小屋

　　"蒙古包"这一称谓源自满语，意为"蒙古人的家或屋"，汉语文献中称之为"穹庐"。牧民定居之后，蒙古包逐渐成为蒙古人游牧时代的历史记忆。图为某蒙古族营地的小屋。

**Mongolian Camp · Hut**
Mongolians call the yurt "Menggubao", meaning "Mongolian home or house". Since the herdsmen settled into permanent housing, the yurt has gradually become a historical memory of the Mongolian nomadic era. The sketch shows a yurt and an attached log cabin of a Mongolian camp.

### 蒙古族营地·室外厨房

　　蒙古族的日常生活大部分都在蒙古包内进行。在空间使用上，蒙古包有严格的功能区划分，兼具卧室、仓库、待客、厨房等多种功能。天气暖和的时候，厨房一般设置于蒙古包外。图为某蒙古族营地的室外厨房。

### Mongolian Camp · Outdoor Kitchen

The yurts are where Mongolian daily-life activities are carried out. But in warm weather, the kitchen is usually set up outside. This sketch shows an outdoor kitchen in Mongolian camp.

图瓦人民居·村落

　　图瓦人是蒙古族的一支,汉语文献中称之为"乌梁海人"。目前人口有2900多人,主要居住在喀纳斯及其周围的白哈巴和禾木村等地。图瓦人的村落位于湖边台地,既与狩猎、捕捞、采摘的生产方式有关,又体现了"藏风聚气"的传统营造观。图为图瓦人民居的村落。

## Tuwa Dwelling House · Village

Tuwa is a branch of the Mongolian ethnic group; the current population of more than 2,900, mainly live in Kanas and the surrounding Haba and Hemu village areas. Tuwa villages are located on lakeside plateaus because lifestyle of hunting, fishing and gathering. The sketch shows a Tuwa village.

图瓦人民居·建筑

图瓦人民居建筑的外墙、屋梁、棚顶、地板等结构多以当地盛产的木材为原料,木与木之间使用卯榫结构联接,圆木相叠的地方用草泥或苔藓来抹缝,保温性能良好,其建筑样式被称作"井干式"。图为图瓦人民居的建筑。

## Tuwa House · Architecture

The walls, roofs, beams, floors and other structures of the Tuwa house, are mostly of abundant local wood joined with mortise and tenon. The gap between logs are filled with grass or moss. The sketch shows the typical architecture of a Tuwa house.

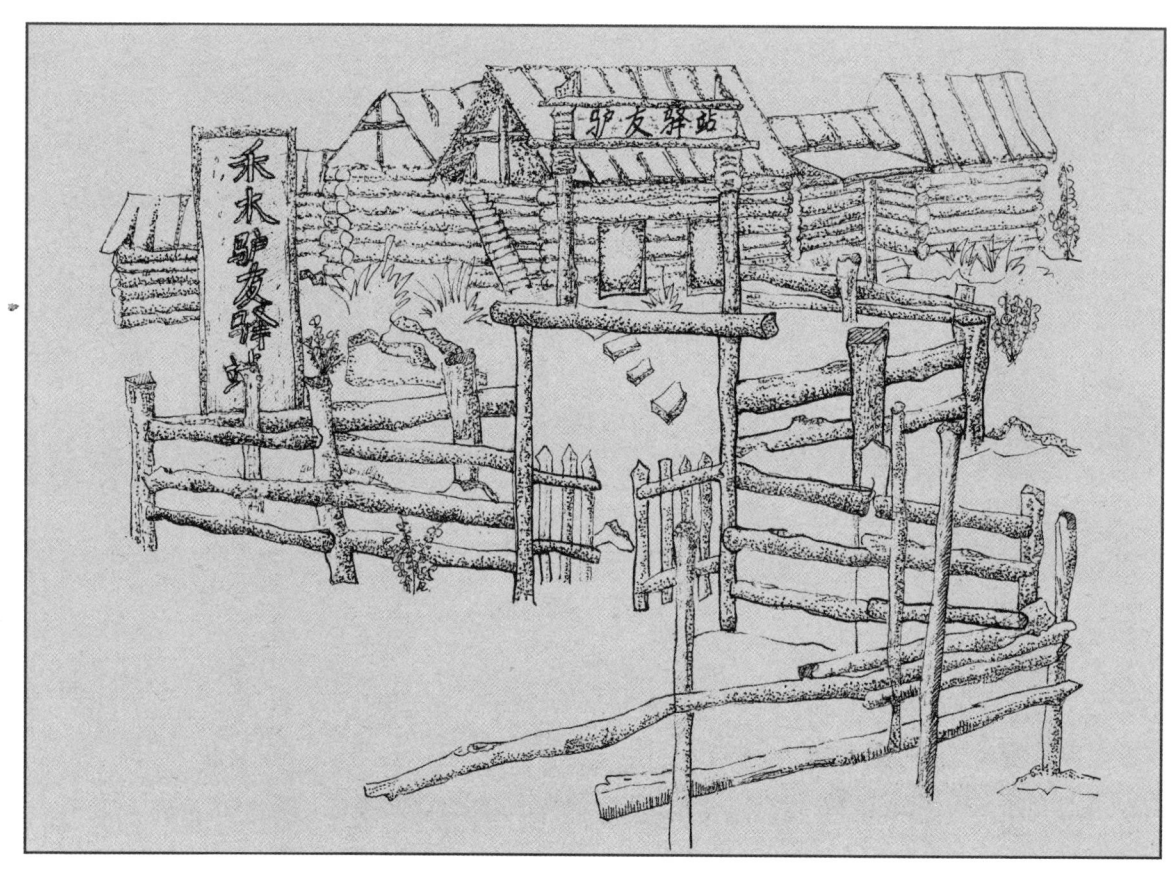

图瓦人民居·院子

　　图瓦人民居建筑的平面多为正方形，门旁仅开一小窗，形成了较为封闭的房间结构。该图为禾木村景区根据传统的图瓦人建筑样式修建的"禾木驴友驿站"。该景区的商店、餐厅、酒店等也均采用这一建筑样式。图为图瓦人民居的院子。

**Tuwa House · Yard**
Tuwa houses are mostly square, with a small window next to the door, forming a relatively closed space. The sketch shows a house with the traditional courtyard style of Tuva architecture.

地窝子·近景

地窝子是兵团初创时期,军垦战士在垦荒造田的间隙,就地取材而创造出的一种过度性建筑形式,这种简单的栖身之所在20世纪70年代初迅速被连队军营式平房所取代。图为某地窝子的近景。

**Low-Lying Hut · Close View**
Constructed by the army to reclaim wasteland, low-lying huts were originally a transitional architectural form that were replaced by bungalows in 1970s. The sketch is a close view of such a hut.

地窝子·大门

　　从建筑形制上来说，地窝子为一种半地穴式建筑。其建造技术简单，工艺粗糙，所用的材料原始，但包含了房屋基本的梁架结构、屋脊、门、墙，讲究一点的地窝子还留出了窗户的位置。图为某地窝子的大门。

**Low-Lying Hut · Door**
A low-lying hut is a semi-crypt-like building containing basic structures like beam, roof, door, and wall. The sketch shows a door of a typical low-lying hut.

地窝子·大门

地窝子一般由军垦战士自己挖掘、自己搭建，最初一个地窝子一般住两人，也有住多人的地窝子，后来战士将其作为婚房。除了居住的地窝子外，还有食堂、菜窖、马厩、库房、会议室等不同功能的地窝子。图为某地窝子的大门。

Low-Lying Hut · Barrack
Low-lying huts are generally built by soldiers for soldiers, but were later used as marriage houses. They served other purposes than just living quarters. The sketch shows the barrack near a low-lying hut.

### 干打垒房子

"干打垒"是一种在两块固定的木板之间填入黏土并夯实的筑墙技术。这座干打垒房子的功能较为齐全,有床铺、火炉、饭桌、长条凳、晾衣绳、行李台等。

### Rammed-Clay-Wall House

Rammed-clay-wall" is a type of wall-building technology by which clay is rammed into the space between fixed wooden plank walls to form a clay wall once the clay is dry and the planks are removed.

# 民风民俗
## Folk Customs

### 逛巴扎的人

"巴扎"是维吾尔语,意为"集市、农贸市场"。在新疆的民族聚居地区,差不多每个乡镇、交通路口,都有巴扎。在缺少电话、电视、报纸、图书的传统社会,逛巴扎是获知生产、手工业、商业信息、外界知识的主要渠道。图为巴扎上交谈的维吾尔族老人。

### Bazaar

A "bazaar" can also be called a "fair" or a "farmers' market". In the Xinjiang Uygur Autonomous Region there are bazaars in almost every town or near major traffic junctions. In traditional society, a bazaar is the main venue for production information, handicrafts, and business. The sketch shows an elderly Uygur man at a bazaar.

### 逛巴扎的人

过去，维吾尔族农民喜欢赶着毛驴车去逛巴扎，大的巴扎甚至会聚集上万辆毛驴车，小的巴扎也会聚集上千辆。如今，交通方式变得日益多样，有人会选择骑马、骑骆驼、骑自行车，还有人会选择公共汽车、摩托车、汽车等现代化交通方式去逛巴扎。

### Bazaar

Uygur farmers traditionally drove their donkey carts to the bazaar. But, nowadays, means of transportation include horse, camel, bike, bus, motorcycle, or car.

> 修鞋匠

　　在乡村的巴扎上，会有修鞋匠专门从事修鞋或者缝补事务，这既是一种谋生的手段，也给维吾尔人的日常生活带来了方便。

## Cobblers
Village bazaars feature cobblers doing shoe repair.

### 打铁匠

维吾尔族铁器制作多采用家庭作坊式，其生产多在自己的住宅庭院中，其销售多集中在乡村或城镇沿街的店铺中。产品有坎土曼、乌修尔镰刀等。

### Blacksmith

Uygur iron production is usually done in family workshops in their own courtyard, with sales at the village and town street shops. Products include Ukraine mattock, Wu Xiuer sickle among others. The sketch is of a Uygur blacksmith.

### 转场队伍

转场一般发生在季节转换时,例如春天冰雪融化之时,牧民要将牲畜从冬窝子转移到夏窝子;冬季大雪来临之前,牧民要将牲畜从夏窝子转移到冬窝子。传统的转场过程非常辛苦,而且因为天气、疾病等方面的原因,充满了风险与苦难。图为某转场队伍。

### Seasonal Transition Team
Seasonal transition generally is very arduous, full of risks and suffering because of weather, disease and other factors. This sketch shows a transition team.

转场牧民

哈萨克族转场的习俗已经持续了1000多年。夏窝子一般位于山前平原地带或盆地中,冬窝子一般位于深山中。除了牲畜要从夏窝子迁移到冬窝子,一同转移的还有牧民维持生活的所有财产以及父母、妻子、孩子等。图为某转场的牧民。

## Seasonal Transition Herdsmen

During the transition, the herdsmen move their livestock from the summer encampment to the winter one, along with their parents, wives, children, property. The sketch shows the transition herdsmen.

### 牧民与马

马是哈萨克族的四大家畜之一，被称作"哈萨克人的翅膀"。其马文化非常丰富，既有驯马、相马、调养快马、赛马、马具制作等与马相关的技艺、体育、娱乐活动，还有与马相关的词汇、谚语以及知识和经验。图为某哈萨克牧民和他的马。

### Herdsmen and Horses
Known as the "wings of the Kazak", horses are one of the four livestock types of a Kazak family. Horse culture is colorful, and includes horse-related skills, sports, recreational activities, vocabulary and knowledge. The sketch shows a typical Kazak herdsman and his horse.

**骑马少年**

哈萨克族被称作"马背上的民族",马在日常的游牧生产、生活和文化中具有举足轻重的作用。马既可以作为交通运输的工具,还是重要的食物;既可以用于战争、狩猎、迁徙,还可以用于娱乐、休闲。图为某哈萨克族的骑马少年。

**Teenagers on Horseback**

The Kazak are called " The people on horseback" because horses play a pivotal role in their daily nomadic production, life and culture. The sketch shows a Kazak teenager on horseback.

驯鹰人

鹰是维吾尔族的图腾之一,他们视鹰为神灵的化身,能够驱邪逐魔。维吾尔族喜欢用鹰的翎毛和尾羽来装饰服饰,用鹰的翅骨来制作鹰笛,模仿鹰的动作而创造出了鹰舞。在偏远地区,有人生病时,鹰被放入室内以祛病消灾。图为维吾尔族驯鹰人。

## Eagle Tamer
Eagles are one of the Uygur totems, regarded as the embodiment of the gods. Uygurs like to use eagle tail feathers to decorate costumes, make flutes with eagle bones, and imitate eagle actions in their dances. This sketch shows a Uygur eagle tamer.

筛谷物的人

粮食种植是北疆农业人口的主要生产方式。北疆冬天寒冷，粮食多以一年一熟为主，只有东部地区可在收获早熟小麦后，再种植早熟玉米或者特早熟大豆，从而实现一年两熟。图为用筛谷物的妇女。

## Woman Sieving Grain

Grain production is the main agricultural activity for people in Northern Xinjiang. Because of the cold winter climate, there is only a single yearly harvest. The sketch shows a woman separating grain from the chaff using a sieve.

### 养蜂人

伊犁河谷的蜜源植物非常丰富，蜂蜜质量和数量都居新疆首位，被称作"塞外蜜库"，每年这里都集中了大量的养蜂人。其中尼勒克县的黑蜂蜜最为驰名，已形成知名度较高的品牌。图为唐布拉草原上的养蜂人。

### Beekeepers

In Yili valley, nectar plants are abundant and the quality and quantity of honey rank highest in Xinjiang: so, many beekeepers are centered here. The sketch shows a beekeeper on Tangbula Grassland.

蜂　房

新疆盛产蜂蜜，主要原因在于蜜源丰富，有杏花、苹果花、油葵花、油菜花、槐花，以及草原上丰富的野花。养蜂人每年3月下旬离家，辗转天山南北，至中秋才回。每个养蜂人大约有100万只蜜蜂，年产蜂蜜10吨左右。图为唐布拉草原上的蜂房。

### Bee Hive

Xinjiang is rich in honey, because of its abundant nectar resources. Beekeepers leave home in March, moving from north to south, only coming back for the Mid-Autumn Festival. Each beekeeper owns about a million bees, with an annual area output of approximately 10 tons of honey. The sketch shows hives on Tangbula Grassland.

### 制奶酒

每年的6～9月是牛的产乳期，图瓦人在这一段时间会将多余的牛奶酿制成奶酒。从牛奶中依次提取了酸奶、酥油、奶豆腐之后，将酒曲加入滤出的乳清中，总共发酵七天左右，经过蒸馏就可以酿制出奶酒。图为制奶酒的人。

### Making Milk Wine

June to September each year is the period for milk production, when Tuva people brew the extra milk into milk wine. The sketch shows people making milk wine.

### 喝奶酒

蒙古语将奶酒译作"赛林艾日哈",成吉思汗将其称作"御膳酒"。在喜庆之时向贵宾和长者敬献哈达和奶酒,是图瓦人最高的待客礼节。图瓦人手工酿造的奶酒酒精度数不到20度,清冽爽口,略带酸味和奶香味,旅游者称其为"腿软酒"。奶酒有改善血液循环,增强免疫力之功效。

### Making Milk Wine

During celebrations, offering the elderly Hada and milk wine is the highest hospitality etiquette for the Tuva. This hand-made milk wine, with an alcohol content of less than 20%, clean and refreshing, slightly sour and with a milk flavor, can improve blood circulation and enhance immunity.

奶酒的仪式

图瓦人酿造奶酒有特殊的仪式，在首次酿造奶酒的灶火上要添加爬山松，再用点燃的爬山松熏灶台、木桶和盛酒的容器，以示祈福。酿出的奶酒要先取上一勺泼在火中，以示尊重灶火，祈福平安。之后再往自家供奉的佛像上洒一点，以示祭拜。同时请来左右邻居一同品尝奶酒，并由德高望重的老人弹酒以敬奉天地。

### People Filling Milk Wine

For Tuva people, brewing milk wine requires a special ceremony, using incense, wine casks, and containers on the fire for the first brewed milk, which is sprinkled into the fire with a spoon and then to the Buddha, whom they worship. Folk invite their neighbors to enjoy the wine with them. The sketch shows people enjoying milk wine.

> 敖包祭祀

  敖包祭祀是蒙古族的标志性文化形态。"敖包"为蒙古语，意为"堆子"。敖包祭祀的崇拜对象是山林、怪石、险峰、树木等狩猎的自然环境。敖包祭祀具有显著的游牧狩猎文化特征。图为敖包祭祀时的某场所。

## Oboo Ritual

The Oboo is a Mongolian symbolic cultural ritual. The objects of worship are grotesque rocks, perilous peaks, trees and other natural elements with distinctive nomadic hunting-culture characteristics. The sketch shows a typical location of oboo ritual.

### 婚礼

　　哈萨克族婚礼中包含了众多的民俗事象，例如仪式、婚礼歌等。婚礼一般分为两个步骤，即女方家送亲礼和婆家迎新礼。大部分仪式均按照伊斯兰教的教规举行，也掺杂一些本民族长期形成的古老习俗。比较有名的婚礼歌有《劝嫁歌》《哭别歌》《揭面纱歌》等。图为某行进中的哈萨克族婚礼队伍。

### Weddings
Kazak weddings feature many folk customs, rituals, wedding songs and so on. Weddings are generally divided into two steps - the bride accompanied by her family and bride escorted by the groom's family, mostly in accordance with Islamic law and some local traditions. The sketch shows the Kazak family wedding party procession.

麦西热甫

　　"麦西热甫"为维吾尔语,汉意为"聚会""场所",是一种集民间音乐、民间舞蹈、乐器演奏、竞技游戏等多种娱乐内容于一身的综合性群众文化活动和文化空间。图为人们在麦西热甫上跳舞。

**Meshrep**

Meaning "gathering place", Meshrep is a comprehensive location for mass cultural activities, such as folk music, folk dance, music performances, competitive games and other entertainments. The sketch shows people dancing on the Meshrep.

且力西

"且力西"为维吾尔语,意为"搏斗"或"较量",是一种维吾尔族的竞技类民俗体育活动。比赛一般采用三局两胜制,主要动作有扛、勾、拌脚等,多在节日、喜庆日、聚会、郊游等场合举行。

## Challenging

Meaning "wrestling" or "contest", Challenging is a kind of Uygur sports activity. Mostly for festivals, celebrations, parties, picnics, the game uses the best of three contests, with the main skills of carrying, dragging, and blocking.

### 斗 羊

斗羊是维吾尔族乡村中的古老的闲暇体育项目和动物竞技项目。在民俗节日和喜庆活动中，维吾尔人都会组织斗羊活动。该活动对场地、设施条件的依赖度不高，只需要一面指挥用的彩旗即可，羊多是自家羊圈里的羊，多由村民自发组织。图为某维吾尔族男子和他的羊。

### Sheep-Fighting

This is the favorite men's leisure and animal sport in the Uygur rural area for festivals and celebrations. The sketch shows a Uygur man and his sheep.

### 仪礼歌

对于哈萨克族来说，人生礼仪中的歌包含了丰富的人文道德、社会风俗、思想感情等方面的知识。人生礼仪中的歌见证了一个人从出生、学会走路、上马到成人、结婚、生子、去世的整个过程。代表作品有《摇篮歌》《婚礼歌》《挽歌》等。图为某哈萨克族妇女在演唱歌曲。

### Ritual Song

For the Kazak, the ritual song for one's life includes a wealth of humanity, morals, social custom, thought, feelings and other aspects of knowledge. It includes the entire process of a person: birth, childhood, adulthood, marriage, having children, and death. The sketch shows a Kazak woman singing.

### 奎 依

"奎依"即哈萨克族的民间器乐曲，一般指用冬不拉、库布孜、斯布孜额等乐器演奏的器乐曲。历史上流传下来的奎依共有几千首，最著名的是《六十二阔恩尔》。

### Kuiyi

A Kazak instrumental music, Kuiyi generally refers to the music played by Tamboura, Kubuz, Sibuze and other folk music instruments. Thousands of songs have been handed down through history.

### 卡拉角勒哈

　　"卡拉角勒哈"为哈萨克语，意为"黑色的走马"，简称"黑走马"。卡拉角勒哈是一种即兴式、自娱性的民间舞蹈，有独舞、对舞、群舞等多种形式。

### Karajurha

Meaning "galloping black horse", Karajurha is a kind of improvisational, entertainment folk dance, including solo, paired, and group dancing.

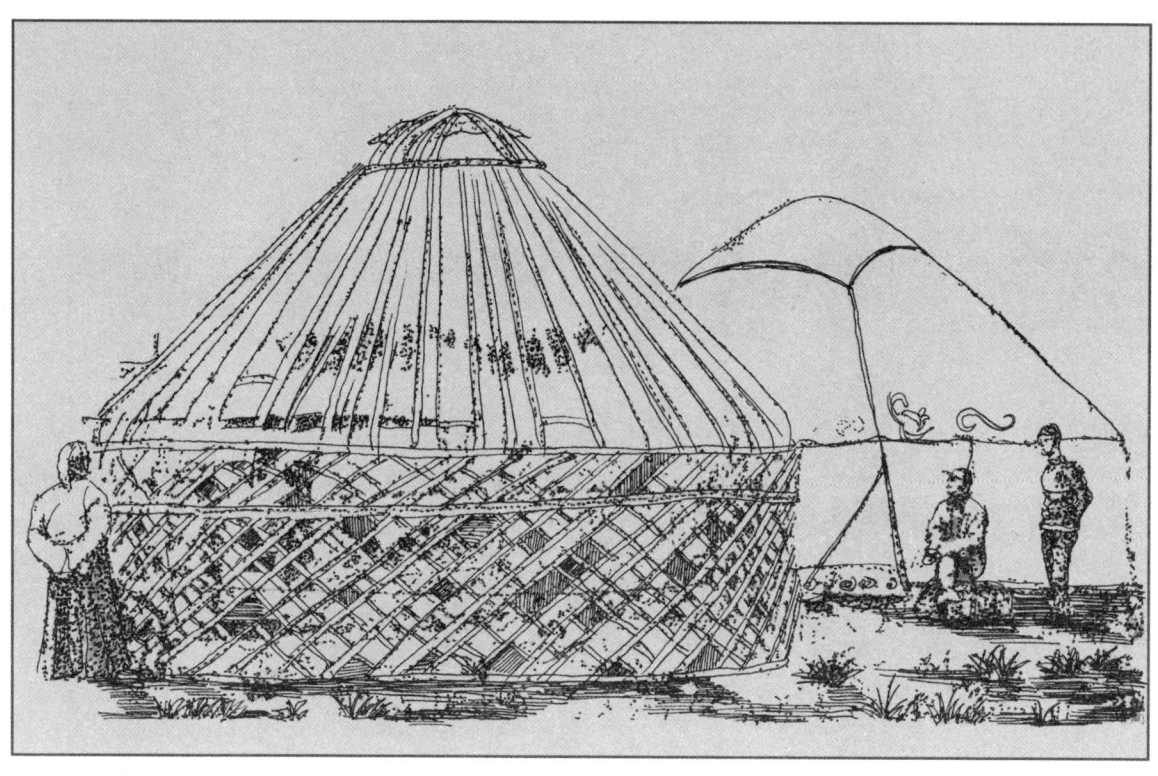

### 哈萨克族毡房制作技艺

　　毡房是哈萨克族日常生活的重要空间，也是其家居文化的综合体现。毡房的主要结构有栅栏杆、毡墙、房顶杆、圈顶、地毯、木门等。毡房由可自由拆卸的上、下两部分组成，上部呈穹隆形，下部呈圆柱形。毡房高度一般在三米左右，面积从二三十平方米到100平方米不等。图为正在搭建的毡房。

### Kazak Yurt Building Skills

The main parts of a yurt are the fence, felt wall, roof pole, circle top, carpet, and wooden doors. Yurts are composed of upper and lower detachable parts - the upper dome-shaped, the lower cylindrical. The sketch shows a yurt under construction.

### 刺绣技艺·维吾尔族

维吾尔族刺绣的风格和内容因地区不同而表现出较大的差异。哈密地区深受中原文化的影响,喜欢使用牡丹、莲、梅等花卉纹,其他维吾尔族聚居区的妇女则喜欢使用巴旦木、石榴、月亮花、神树纹等植物图案。图为某维吾尔族妇女在做刺绣。

**Uygur Embroidery Skills**

Uygur embroidery style and content vary from region to region. Hami style features peony, lotus, plum and other flower patterns, while the style of other areas showcases the Palestinian Danwood, pomegranate, moon flower, divine tree and other plant patterns. The sketch shows a Uygur woman doing embroidery.

### 刺绣技艺·哈萨克族

　　哈萨克族刺绣可分为毡绣、布绣、皮革绣等种类，多用来装饰挂毯、地毯、箱套、帷帐、门帘、窗帘、桌布、枕套等日常生活用品或服饰。图为某哈萨克族妇女在做刺绣。

**Embroidery Skills · Kazak**

By different characteristics, Kazak embroidery can be divided into felt embroidery, cloth embroidery, leather embroidery and other types, mostly for decorating tapestries, carpets, boxes, bed curtains, door curtains, window curtains, tablecloths, pillowcases and other daily necessities or clothing. The sketch shows a Kazak woman doing embroidery.

【刺绣技艺·蒙古族】

　　蒙古族刺绣在工具、针法、风格等方面与其他民族刺绣有着显著的差异，针法质朴粗犷，色彩对比强烈，喜爱贴花，追求肌理感。

## Embroidery Skills · Mongolian

Mongolian embroidery is designated as a national non-material cultural heritage. Its style is rough, with strong color contrast and many appliques.

### 帕拉斯制作技艺

　　帕拉斯制作技艺是蒙古族的传统技艺，即毛线编织。编织品可用来制作蒙古包、大衣、床铺、马鞍、褡裢等。该图为帕拉斯的第一个步骤——捻毛线，用一根棍转，就可以将羊毛或驼毛捻成毛线。

### Palas Making Skill

Palas, wool weaving, is a Mongolian traditional skill. The sketch shows the first step — twist yarn, turn with a stick, and twist the wool or camel hair into woolen yarn.

### 红柳条编织技艺

　　维吾尔族红柳条编织的主要材料为沙漠地区生长的红柳枝条，用来编织各类生产、生活用品以及用于陈设的手工艺品，有接近2000年的历史。图为某维吾尔族男子在编筐。

**Red Wicker Weaving Skills**
The main Uygur weaving material is the desert area's red willow branches that can be used to weave all kinds of articles for production and life, daily necessities and handicrafts. The sketch shows a Uygur man weaving baskets.

### 维吾尔族长辫子

维吾尔族姑娘有留长辫子的习俗。小女孩从三岁开始留头发,将头发梳成数量不等的小辫子,最少的有五六条,最多的可达三四十条。图为梳着长辫子的维吾尔族姑娘。

### Uygur Long Braids

After the 17th century, Uygur girls developed the custom of wearing long braids. After the age of three, little girls do not cut their hair, but comb it into several small pigtails, numbering from at least five or six, to thirty or forty. The sketch shows a Uygur girl with long braids.

### 可依米塞克头饰

哈萨克族妇女佩戴的头饰。该头饰为白色，由头套和披肩两部分组成，披肩上绣羊角纹和几何纹。这种头巾用的布大而宽，可遮住头、肩和腰部，直达臀部以下。戴上以后，只露出眼睛、嘴巴和鼻子。年长妇女戴的头巾没有花纹和图案，年纪较轻的戴的，则在胸前、头顶上都绣有图案和花纹。

### Keyimisek Headdress

This is the headdress of Kazak women. The white headdress is composed of two parts: the hijab, and a shawl with horn and geometric patterns. Elderly women wear hijabs without patterns, while young women's hijabs are embroidered with patterns on the chest and the head.